Colonel William D'Alton Mann

Elbert Hubbard

Kessinger Publishing's Rare Reprints

Thousands of Scarce and Hard-to-Find Books
on These and other Subjects!

- Americana
- Ancient Mysteries
- Animals
- Anthropology
- Architecture
- Arts
- Astrology
- Bibliographies
- Biographies & Memoirs
- Body, Mind & Spirit
- Business & Investing
- Children & Young Adult
- Collectibles
- Comparative Religions
- Crafts & Hobbies
- Earth Sciences
- Education
- Ephemera
- Fiction
- Folklore
- Geography
- Health & Diet
- History
- Hobbies & Leisure
- Humor
- Illustrated Books
- Language & Culture
- Law
- Life Sciences

- Literature
- Medicine & Pharmacy
- Metaphysical
- Music
- Mystery & Crime
- Mythology
- Natural History
- Outdoor & Nature
- Philosophy
- Poetry
- Political Science
- Science
- Psychiatry & Psychology
- Reference
- Religion & Spiritualism
- Rhetoric
- Sacred Books
- Science Fiction
- Science & Technology
- Self-Help
- Social Sciences
- Symbolism
- Theatre & Drama
- Theology
- Travel & Explorations
- War & Military
- Women
- Yoga
- *Plus Much More!*

**We kindly invite you to view our catalog list at:
http://www.kessinger.net**

Colonel William D'Alton Mann

WHAT has become of Colonel William D'Alton Mann? *○ *○

Six months ago the Sunday Sewer had his picture on the front page and gave columns to his crimes, trying to kill him with sewer gas. One famous Cigarettist said he would never rest until the Colonel was in Sing Twice, his white whiskers shaved clean and his martial form covered with a baggy suit of prison gray, because, forsooth, the Colonel has sworn it happened on the Tuesda' when bigum it was on the Thursda'.

Justice!

For weeks the newspaper pack hunted, hooted, jibed, jeered, reviled and spit upon Colonel Mann.

It made one think of the good old days in England when naked women were whipped through the streets at the cart's tail. What were these women guilty of? No one knew. Did the mob that pelted them with mud know them? Not at all—the mob spirit was rampant, that was all.

And so the mob spirit occasionally breaks out with us yet and finds its expression of brutality in the newspapers. That is why I refer to the average daily paper as a sewer—do you see the application? And in this sense it may be a necessity. We have refined our bestiality to a point where we merely relish reveling in it in print; we roll it as a sweet morsel under our tongues, and toss it back and forth over the teacups.

Newspapers are business ventures, and newspaper editions are just a very little worse than newspaper readers. The newspaper owners are panderers to the mob spirit, they do in cold blood what the reader does subconsciously. Editors and writers differ from owners because they frankly admit, out of office hours, the rottenness of the product, but they have to live, even if

James McNeill Whistler could n't see the necessity. Not one reader in a million dare affront Colonel Mann if they met face to face, but we enjoy seeing the editor, hiding behind anonymity, vent his rheum upon him in print.

The owner of an average daily paper is a direct descendant of the Impenitent Thief, the most prepotent man in history.

A private character is no more to a newspaper manager, than were the feelings of the naked woman at the cart's tail to the London mob nor the anguish of Hester Prynne with the scarlet letter on her breast as she held little Pearl to her heart in the blaze of the market place, to the hypocrites who called themselves Christians.

The State no longer pillories Hester Prynne in the Market place— it simply delegates the task to the Daily Dope, which we so feverishly munch ere we can begin the business of the day.

¶ This is the third paragraph I have recently written telling what I think of the daily paper. Only one paper in America has printed the Warm Stuff and replied to it without beginning and ending by telling what a bad man I am, and that was the Denver *Post*. This paper published my article and its reply and has since issued them together in a pamphlet that can be secured for the postage. Dozens of other papers replied to me, however, and the way they did it was by confining their argument closely to what they are pleased to call my personal history, calling on their imaginations for their facts.

When you can not answer your opponent's logic, do not be discouraged—you can still call him vile names.

Possibly the best example in present times of the mob spirit finding an accommodating vent through the daily press was the case of Maxim Gorky.

Gorky, a writer of much power, and an unselfish and honest man, came to this country a political exile from his native land. His errand here was one of mercy—he was pleading the cause of

Freedom. His route had been laid out across the continent, and meetings were arranged where he was to state the case of men struggling in bonds.

Suddenly a New York newspaper with lurid headlines fired a broadside to the effect that the woman traveling with Mr. Gorky was not his wife. And lo! from Maine to Oregon and from the Gulf of Mexico to Lake Superior the newspapers took up the cry. Gorky's work in America was paralyzed; the people he hoped to meet here he could not see; he was driven from his hotel in New York City, and private charity only served to protect him from the storm.

Later, it turned out that the woman traveling with Mr. Gorky was his wife, and was so recognized by the State and Society in Russia ﾟﾟ ﾟﾟ

Now coming back to the point of beginning I ask, who is this Colonel W. D. Mann, whom the blessed newspapers of the land used for a door-mat for a whole week, or until Gorky took his place in the stocks and in turn was pelted with rubbish—who is Colonel Mann?

As the newspapers did n't tell, I will, although right here I want to say I do not know the gentleman personally; and so far as I know none of his near friends are mine; moreover I have never subscribed nor bought a copy of either of his silly publications. My interest in him arose from the damning count made by the New York *World,* thus: " All of his property is in his daughter's name! " ﾟﾟ ﾟﾟ

That struck me as pretty good; evidently Colonel Mann has faith in his daughter—he must love her, and she loves him. The man surely is n't half bad. Do you remember that classic of the old man who was condemned to starve in prison being suckled by his daughter? Do you remember the tale of Cordelia and King Lear? Do you remember the love of Madam de Stael for her father, Jacques Neckar?

And so I looked up ol' man Mann, and found he was born in Sandusky, Ohio, in 1839; and worked his way through Lima College; educating himself for a civil engineer. When the war broke out he was twenty-one years old. He entered the volunteer army in the First Michigan Cavalry. In 1862 he organized the Fifth Michigan Cavalry and was made a Captain. The same year, on personal request of the Governor he organized the Seventh Michigan Cavalry—sometimes known as the " Invincible Seventh," and led them in many battles. He was several times wounded and was mentioned by Siegel for valiant service, and endorsed by Lincoln in a list of names of men who deserved special recognition for personal bravery in time of action.

Colonel Mann has been granted sixteen patents for military accoutrements, some of which are now used by the Government. He was granted twenty-eight patents for railway appliances. He is the inventor of the Mann Boudoir Car and the organizer of the company that built these cars. In 1883 this company was absorbed by the Pullman Company and Colonel Mann suddenly found himself floundering in the mulligatawney. His worst offence seems to be that he has successfully " touched " Pierpont Morgan, Perry Belmont and Astorbilt—all Smart Setters— without sufficient collateral.

All the men who tried to submerge Mann in the muck of their minds tried the artistic touch on these same parties that he touched, without success. As near as I can get at it, the money he borrowed from them, they first stole from him—giving him the double cross, or I should say the financial cross-buttock. If any blame should be sent Mann's way it should be because he let 'em off so easy. On this score his conscience should certainly trouble him, and remorse should gnaw at his gizzard.